India

Himalayan Sanctuaries

Stephen and Scharlie Platt

www.leveretpublishing.com

India: Himalayan Sanctuaries
First published - July 2017
Published by
Leveret Publishing
56 Covent Garden, Cambridge, CB1 2HR, UK

Warli painting (photo Shruti Harohalli)

ISBN 978-0-9957680-8-6

India

Himalayan Sanctuaries

Dharanasi Pass, Nanda Devi 4300m (photo Michael Green)

India 2006

UTTARAKHAND
CHINA
NEW DELHI
NEPAL
INDIA

UTTARAKHAND
TOURIST MAP
N
HIMACHAL PRADESH
Govind Pashu National Park
Yamuna
Bhagirathi
Yamunotri
Gangotri
NH-58
CHINA
INDIA
Uttarkashi
Paunthi
NH-134
NH-108
Kedarnath
Rambada
Valley of Flowers
Joshimath
Alaknanda
Mussoorie
Tehri Garhwal
Guptkashi
Chamoli
Ghansali
Nanda Devi Bioshpere Reserve
Gochar
Devprayag
Pauri
NH-58
NH-119
Rishikesh
Ganges
Tharali
Gwaldom
National Park
Haridwar
Lansdowne
Bageshwar
Kali
NEPAL
Dugadda
Mirai Malli
NH-74
Jim Corbett National Park
Ranikhet
Almora
Pithoragarh
UTTAR PRADESH
LEGEND
National Highway
Major Road
Railway
District Boundary
State Boundary
International Bdy
River
Other Town
Major Town
Tourist Places
Religious Places
Nainital
Bhimtal
Lohaghat
Champawat
NH-74
Jaspur
Kashipur
Haldwani
Ramganga
Tanakpur
Rudrapur
Sitarganj
Map not to Scale
Copyright © 2015 www.mapsofindia.com
(Updated on 20th January 2015)

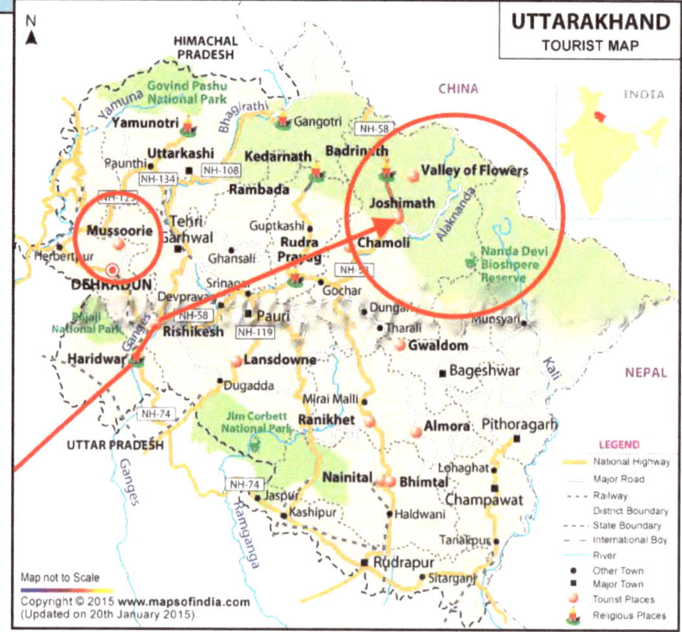

Delhi

Sunday 3 September

We fly from Heathrow. It is four weeks since a bomb scare and the queue for security snakes all the way through the shopping area along endless corridors and all the way into the car park. The main bottleneck is the scanner. Two Indian ladies are ahead of us. Their handbags and vanity cases are full of make-up and perfume and they let out squeals of dismay as the security man confiscates one item after another, saying haven't you seen the news during the last three weeks. They both lose large bottles of Gaviscon digestive medicine, but they let out the biggest wail when their compacts are confiscated. Don't be like that, one of them said in tears horrified at the thought of arriving in Delhi unable to repair the ravages of the flight.

We take a taxi to the Connaught Hotel and get a good rest after arriving about midday. We set off walking to Connaught Circus but are accosted by a chuk chuk driver – a jovial tubby bearded Sikh who persuades Phil and Anna to let him take us. His daughter is studying hotel management in London, he says.

Connaught Circus, New Delhi

All four of us squeeze in. He says most of the bazaars were closed on Sunday, but took us to a four-storey emporium just around the corner. All the buildings here look ramshackled so we didn't immediately grasp his intentions. We got no further than the first carpet shop where a delightful man introduced himself and said he came from a weaver's family. He invited us to sit on one of the sofas while he told us how the carpets were made. He explained the process with the aid of a small loom and said the best carpets had 400 knots per square inch. He said he was from Kashmir, where the carpets were made, and asked if we'd like tea. He showed us how the carpet was made by tying figure-of-eight knots in a pair of strings. A piece of yarn was pulled down and knotted through the strings and then cut off with a hooked knife. After each row had been completed the knots were hammered to compact them for a full minute or so with a tool like a bear's claw with a dozen steel spikes. The horizontal bar was pulled down again and the strings reversed for the next row of knots.

The man explained how the tradition came from Persia, but had been adapted in Kashmir from designs in books. The design for a carpet is coloured

Anna gets a lesson in carpet making

onto graph paper. Colours are chosen and the design transferred onto strips of brown card in which each block of colour was represented by a symbol – the weavers' language. He kept up a continuous patter about what a good investment this type of carpet would be. He told us about the natural dyes made from nuts, roots and leaves collected in the jungle. He spoke about the process of washing and drying the carpets in the sun. These carpets are made to be used, he said, the pile gets better if you walk on it, he said. And you remove stains with cut lemon, yoghurt and salt, or potato, and a damp cloth.

Steve was thinking that this is all very interesting, but how am I going to get away without having to buy one. He was relieved when Phil and Anna began to show an interest in a beautiful red and gold tribal rug with long dark tassels formed from strings made from yak wool. By now the man had a boy unroll half a dozen rugs, beginning with a beautiful silk carpet. He showed us how each carpet looked different when turned around. The reason was because the knots lay in one direction. This had the benefit that furniture wouldn't crush the pile like it would on a man-made carpet. Phil and Anna have homed in on one carpet they like and the assistant removes the other carpets, leaving only three or four favoured ones. Scharlie said how much she liked the silk one he had shown us first. The man says, take off your shoes and walk on it in bare feet. Here we go, Steve thought as Scharlie blissfully walked about.

Steve considered all the objections to his buying a carpet and realised the salesman was covering each one. The carpets were kept rolled against the wall and looked huge. But an assistant brought out a small jute package and explained how they folded and wrapped the carpet and got the client to sign their name over each seam to prove that they had got the carpet they had bought. They could take it with them or could have it couriered back home.

Phil and Anna were bargaining him down from his starting price until they settled on less than half. They paid by MasterCard. At least I haven't brought my credit card, thought Steve. Phil and Anna concluded their business and the salesman turned to us with a look in his eye that said you're next. Scharlie said she liked the silk carpet and asked if she could reserve it until tomorrow. Steve said, no way! She asked how much it was. Much less than it would cost in England, he said. Steve agreed it was beautiful, but said that was irrelevant since we couldn't afford it. So he came down again in price, finishing finally at about half the starting price. Steve was still adamant we wouldn't buy, but Scharlie really loved it and wasn't hiding her desire. The salesman said he could try one

The salesman suggest Scharlie take off her shoes and walk barefoot on the silk carpet

more thing. He had reached the limit he could authorise but would talk to his manager. A cultivated man arrived and said that the first and last customers of the day were blessed and that he would give us a good price of £614. Steve could see from Scharlie's face that we wouldn't get out of the shop without buying. So he said okay but I don't have my credit card, ha-ha. No problem, they said, we will come to your hotel.

Two assistants packed up the carpet while we chatted to the manager about politics – he thought Blair to be a weak leader, the mouthpiece of Bush. They sewed our carpet into a canvas bag and Scharlie signed her name across the seams so no one could tamper with it while we were away trekking. This is something I am going to treasure, said Scharlie, kissing Steve. He imagined we'd have a night to sleep on the decision, but the salesman had the VISA slip all made out. An assistant was waiting for us with the card machine when we got back to the hotel, and when the bank wanted authorisation, the salesman arrive and talked to them over the phone.

Scharlie writes her name on the jute parcel containing our carpet

Monday 4 September

Breakfast of pawpaw and croissant, good tea and coffee, and our personal chuck chuck rickshaw waiting for us outside a hotel with a friend in a second vehicle to take us to old Delhi to see the sights. Our driver kept warning us to keep close hold of our belongings and as soon as we reach the crowded streets we were approached by children begging.

Our intrepid driver plays dodgems with other rickshaw drivers, accompanied by the street music of horns and shouting. Mothers with babies, agile and single-minded, stretch out cupped hands for money whenever we slow down. It's hard to deal with the conflicting feelings of pity and irritation. We walk and men try to persuade us to go in one direction or another. A man sitting on the pavement tickles a cobra, which rears its body from the basket. He wants Scharlie to take a photo but she remembers that snakes are becoming rare in the wild and refuses.

The Jama Masjid mosque is the biggest in India and was built by Shah Jahan about 1650. It's made of red sandstone and white marble. You take your shoes off at the entrance before passing through the gatehouse into a

Phil in a chuk chuk venturing forth to explore Delhi

The Jama Masjid mosque is the biggest in India

huge courtyard of red stone flags. There are two minarets bordering an open arcade where people pray. We wandered about chatting, moving from the shade as the sun came out and back into the open as it clouded over. Phil and I examined the construction of one of the gates. It was about 25 foot high and made of overlapping balks of timber about eight inches thick and a foot wide, the vertical and horizontal boards stitched together with iron nails hammered through and bent over. The door was then reinforced with bronze cladding on the outside and horizontal transoms on the inside again nailed through, with the heads of the nails forming the design on the outside metal face of the door.

The Red Fort is close by, and our two drivers hover while we try and take a photo and then follow as we try and walk. They offer to take us to a garden, but they change plans and take us to another emporium. We are keen not

Steve and Phil examine the majestic main door of the mosque

to get inveigled, so we walked back to the hotel, having paid off the drivers.

We meet the rest of the party over lunch in the hotel and Michael gives us the lowdown on plans for the journey. This is the first trek that Michael and Mary have arranged in their new venture Time to Be Off. They met in the Himalayas in 1980 when Michael was doing his PhD research. They invited close friends to join them and two of these friends, Anna and Phil, invited us.

Lunch is excellent and the vegetarian Indian cuisine suits us – tandoori cottage cheese, salad, rice and vegetable bhajis, with fresh limejuice to drink. In the afternoon Scharlie is keen to visit the bazar that Michael told her about where you don't have to haggle. It is a government initiative stocking goods from all over India that's a little more expensive but a lot less tiring. The five-storey bazaar is on Janpath and we walk there by the outer circle. We whisk round to see what they have. Scharlie wants to buy Christmas presents for the children and manages to get some papier maché animals, a T-shirt for Jack, a skirt for Phoebe and a cotton mat for Leveret Croft. After an hour and a half she was wiped out from the heat and longing for the hotel and a shower. Back through the barrage of vendors and beggars a well-spoken young man catches her eye and follows her, trying to sell her a carved cobra. This is good, he says, it

Schoolgirls in Delhi

is hardwood and could be table decoration. All my family make these, we have plenty of work. What is your price? I'm a student and have no money. Where are you from? I have friends in Cambridge, Southampton and Newcastle. Our chuck chuck arrives to take us back to the hotel but before we can get in a man, shuffling rapidly on his knees with twisted legs dragging, approaches us. In perfectly enunciated English and with a cheerful smile, he said, I am a beggar, have you some money? He made it sound a respectable job or work suitable for this situation so we gave him our change.

Steve went to explore the city on his own. He finds the inner circle and goes round once. He thinks about going into what looks like an interesting cake shop called Wenglers when he notices a dollop of shit on his shoe. It's only when reading the guide, back in the hotel, having cleaned his shoe, that he realises he has been a victim of the famous Connaught Place 'shot gun shit on shoe scam' aimed at generating custom for the shoe cleaning wallahs.

The shower is delicious; probably the last we'll get for a couple of weeks and the air-conditioning keeps us cold enough to need blankets. There is drumming in the street and we can see a procession with lights from treelike candelabra. It's a wedding party. The groom is supposed to arrive on a white horse but he emerges from a white car draped in orange webbing like a fly in the spider's web. The women are dancing to the drums and pipes. There are tables set in the garden of the hotel for a couple of hundred people. Scharlie writes her postcards home. She goes down to reception to buy stamps and post them in the hotel. But the glue on them doesn't stick and she has to stick each one down with a glue pot.

Tuesday 5 September

We are down in the lobby before six and manage to grab breakfast of croissant, tea and pawpaw before boarding the taxis to the train station. This is the hardest part of the trip, says Michael, getting everyone and our luggage onto the train. The platform is crowded and porters are pushing handcarts with jute wrapped parcels. But we refuse offers of porterage and manhandle our own bags onto the platform. Having all our stuff in two big bags works well. Mary has the tickets but it takes some time to find out where our seats are. We find we are in the front of the train in executive class. The train is old and battered, but the seats are comfortable and the service excellent. It is aired conditioned but otherwise reminiscent of 1950s trains with lots of space, scratchy music from speakers, lino on the floor and a train horn that sounds high and multi corded.

A uniformed waiter serves us breakfast in stages over the first two hours. We have red-checked gingham napkins. Tea and biscuits followed by cornflakes with hot rich buffalo milk, then vegetable bhajis, carrots and green beans all wrapped in a foil packet. The waiter clears each course away before the next one appears. Finally he serves us with a thermos flask of coffee and a banana. We sip coffee and watch the countryside flow past – a patchwork of maize and cane, ploughed fields and ponds full of monsoon rain. This is a restful way of travelling. We are being broken in gently. The passing countryside is ordered squares of lush green fields of sugar cane and maize criss-crossed by lines of eucalyptus or clumps of popular. Near the villages there are scrubby areas and pools of water with people doing their ablutions amongst white egrets.

Train journey from New Delhi to Haridwar

In Haridwar we struggle down the platform with our bags and are met by our two drivers. The road north is crowded and we seem to drink our way round trucks and carts. We stopped for lunch in Rishikesh, which is a major religious centre on the Ganges, now geared to provide Western tourists with massage and alternative medicine. From here it's only a short distance to our hotel for the night – a complex of chalets built about three years ago as a centre for the rafting business. The stone chalets nestle into a steep wooded hillside. Planting is subtle, merging seamlessly into the surrounding forest. The rooms are beautifully designed and the whole place is delightful. It's called the Himalayan Hideaway. The staff carry our bags down the steep hill and we choose the first room we reach to save them having to carry them further. It is still hot and sticky but the room has an efficient fan and an en-suite bathroom. This is the last luxury we will experience. There is a view down the river and across the valley to steep wooded slopes. We wander down to the river. The path finishes at a sandy beach and we paddle and play ducks and drakes with chunks of slate broken off from the rocks. The current is fast, it's just after the monsoon and the river is full and flowing too fiercely to swim but we sit in the water to cool off. The rest of the group join us and we spend a pleasant

Himalayan Hideaway, Rishikesh

hour chatting.

We go to the main lodge for dinner and sit in the garden watching the sun go down while waiting for the others to join us. The tree frogs remind us of our life in the tropics and through binoculars we watch a peasant family in a small clearing in the forest across the valley. Watching the people move about at the end of the day, the men in dull grey and the women in brown and blue saris, they seemed to be just pottering. Supper was superb – served with in a large main dining room with a choice of many vegetarian dishes and crème caramel and chocolate cake to follow. The three men who serve us stand direct and silent throughout the meal, attentive to our every need.

Wednesday 6 September

We wake refreshed and have a very civilised breakfast. Our Jeeps are waiting for us and it's a long drive to Joshimath at the start of our trek. We are with the older lead driver today and his style is smoother than our driver yesterday. His hands sit relaxed on the steering wheel and his judgement when to overtake or to nip into the side of the road to avoid oncoming vehicle is

Anna, Phil and Steve paddling in the Ganges

faultless. He gives the impression of knowing every inch of the route. Just as well because there are continuous hairpin bends with vertical drops and the occasional landslide. Work gangs cutting stone to repair the embankment are a frequent sight as are women cutting grass. The women load the huge bundles on their backs and seem to walk for miles.

This is the route to the Sikh temple at Hemkund, and we will be joining the throngs of pilgrims and walking the way for two days before going on to the Valley of the Flowers. The road climbs up by the lush valley of the Ganges. We stop by the side of the road to view where the Alaknanda River joins the browner Ganges and watch men bathing in a small ghat at the point where the two rivers meet. It looked exhilarating if not downright dangerous in the strong current.

We stop for lunch at shady roadside services of bamboo and thatch. Two coaches are parked outside and the drivers had spread a huge white plastic on the ground for passengers to sit on and have lunch – the women first and then the men. It all seems very orderly and civilised and reminds us of camping in Spain with the children. We sit at long trestle tables and enjoy the varieties of rice, vegetables and chapattis; a cuisine we don't tire of. Scharlie finds that

Intreped bathers at a ghat where the Alaknanda joiuns the Ganges

sitting in the centre of the back seat is best. The air circulates and she can look straight ahead at the horizon to avoid feeling sick.

We reached Joshimath and found our guide Sanjay at the Mountain View Hotel. There is a presentation about a hydroelectric scheme in the area and Michael takes issue with the engineer, which surprises us because he has been mild and non-confrontational up to now. The young engineer is enthusiastic and defends himself well.

We are staying about a mile above the village in a bungalow built by the trekking company. They plan to build more bungalows but for now there are only beds for couples and the rest of the party are camping. We got one of the three rooms with our own bathroom, which is wonderful even without hot water.

Coach party make a civilised lunch stop by the side of the road

Hemkund

Thursday 7 September

In the morning while we wait to leave Jim and Scharlie wander along the road for a mile identifying plants. They spot fragaria, artemisia, rubus, geranium and a delicate pink polygonum they would have liked to have in England. It brings home to them how much the horticultural world originated from this area. Jim has a nursery in Norfolk that he runs with his wife.

New drivers pick us up. It is a half-hour drive up a beautiful side valley to Govindghat, a settlement with a suspension bridge across the Alaknanda River from where we can see a long trail of pilgrims crawling up the steeply curving path following the Laxman Gorge to Ghangaria, the village where we will stop for the night on our way to the Sikh Gundwara at Hemkund.

Michael is something of a celebrity here and we go to the forest department quarters and are offered tea and biscuits. The cool interior reminds Scharlie

Adventure Treks bungalow in Joshimath and group about to board jeeps

of old houses in Jamaica and it feels like a legacy of the British Raj – ordered, simple and comfortable. We meet an official from the forestry department who will escort us to our campsite. This is his patch and he rules here. Finally we set off just before midday. It is hot, but most of the people have disappeared ahead of us. We plunge down a steep street like entering a cave with cloth hangings stretched to form a roof. Little shops and stalls line the street and the variety and elegance of people's dress, the beautifully arranged foods on sale, the richly patterned shawls and clothes is almost too much to take in.

It is quite a leisurely walk of about eight miles through woodland by the side of a mountain river. The porters carry our gear along with the cooking tent and full paraphernalia to producing proper meals – pilau, dahl, chapattis, soup and porridge for breakfast. The path rises steadily in zigzags and there is tree cover so we are not suffering from the heat. A steady stream of travellers moves with us, many on ponies. Some of those coming down have a glazed look in their eyes as if they are very tired. Every quarter mile there are booths or teashops by the side of the path selling refreshments. The preferred

We plunge down a cave like street with cloth hangings stretched to form a roof.

Soon after leaving Govindghat on the walk up to the Sikh temple at Hemkund

Michael and his sister Alison, Scharlie and pilgrims

Tea shop on the way to Hemkund

A stop at one of the many tea shops on the way

local brew is tea with milk and spices and lots of sugar. We stop at regular intervals and it takes six hours to reach the flat area below Ghangaria. Since leaving Delhi, Michael and Mary pay for the food and treat us at the tea stops. Suddenly Scharlie feels sick and dizzy. We are at 9,000 feet and she's worried its altitude. A recent study, examining altitude sickness, found that a third of the thousands of pilgrims travelling to Hemkund Sahib each year suffered from acute mountain things improved and she reaches the campsite in style.

The campsite is in a lush green field surrounded by heavily wooded cliffs. The Sherpas have chosen a site and erected the tents and Steve has laid out the mats and sleeping bags. We have two mats each – foam mats provided by the trekking company and inflatable mattresses that we brought with us, so we are very comfortable. There is a continuous procession of people on the path. They are going up to the Gundwara, about 4 miles further and 4,000 feet higher at 14,000 feet. People travel in whole families, small babies, venerable old men and women, making their slow way of pilgrimage.

Scharlie feels ill with a cold and she has a fever; we are now at 10,000 feet, the same as in Quito, and she remembers how she felt there. We are

Scharlie meeting family of Sikh pilgrims in campsite below Ghangaria

offered tea and after a wash we have a nice meal of chicken soup followed by vegetable curry. Sanjay organises the porters and the logistics of the whole expedition. He also does the cooking and takes great pride in giving us good local delicacies. The tourist is my god, we are here to please you, he says with grace and humour.

Friday 8 September

We are woken by Sanjay offering us tea in bed. We were deeply asleep and didn't hear and have to be shaken awake. We have plenty of time to wash pack and breakfast before for setting off. Scharlie had been awake coughing in the night. She wants to go up but is feeling too unwell to walk so she and Jim decide to rent ponies. Steve wants to be on his own, figures she will catch him up, and sets off. The ponies are mules that they must have been bred from gentle stock since they are docile and biddable with huge gentle eyes and long eyelashes. But Scharlie's mount is more reluctant than others to move and the pony man has to urge it forward with continuous clicks of his tongue, shouted commands and an occasional swish of his grass whip.

Scharlie and Jim opt for mules on the second day's ascent to Hemkund

After we're gone through the village and crossed the river, Steve gradually leaves the others behind. The path is made of flat stone flags, but every so often there is a steep short cut. You see the same people again and again; they

Sikh pilgrims, Ghangaria

are on ponies and faster, but they stop to rest. Steve's going slow and steady and, because he's hot and doesn't want to catch a chill, he keeps going. He sees Scharlie and Jim coming so he stops and sits on a tree trunk near a bend

Through the mist the loud haunting sound of a huge brass horn encouraging the faithful

so he can photograph them as they ride by. The track zigzags up and Steve starts taking shortcuts. The sun has gone and the mist has come down. As he's reaching the temple complex at the top Scharlie and Jim catch him up.

There are supposed to be spectacular views but we have been in mist all the way up and the lake and the temple are shrouded in cloud; shapes, colours and muffled sounds emerge from the fog. Hemkund means lake of snow, and is fed by melt water. Each pilgrim must bathe in the lake and several men with ample bellies dressed in loincloths and turbans seem to take enjoyment from ducking into the icy water. Their bodies steam and they beam with exhilaration. We take photographs – the Sikhs only too pleased to have their photos taken.

Scharlie is very cold having been sitting on the horse. She is shivering and puts on every possible bit of clothing including Jim's gloves and Steve's anorak. We wander around the temple saying hello to people and walk around the edge of the lake looking at the flowers. A bearded Sikh in a blue tunic is playing a loud haunting sound on a huge brass horn. He says we can't go on and should sit and listen. He blows for a while, then takes the horn apart and uses it to rescue flies from the surface of the lake. Jim asks him if we can take his picture. He's very friendly and gives us sweet peanuts from his pocket.

Scharlie rings the bell at Hemkund

A welcome hot drink at the Hemkund Sikh Gundwara

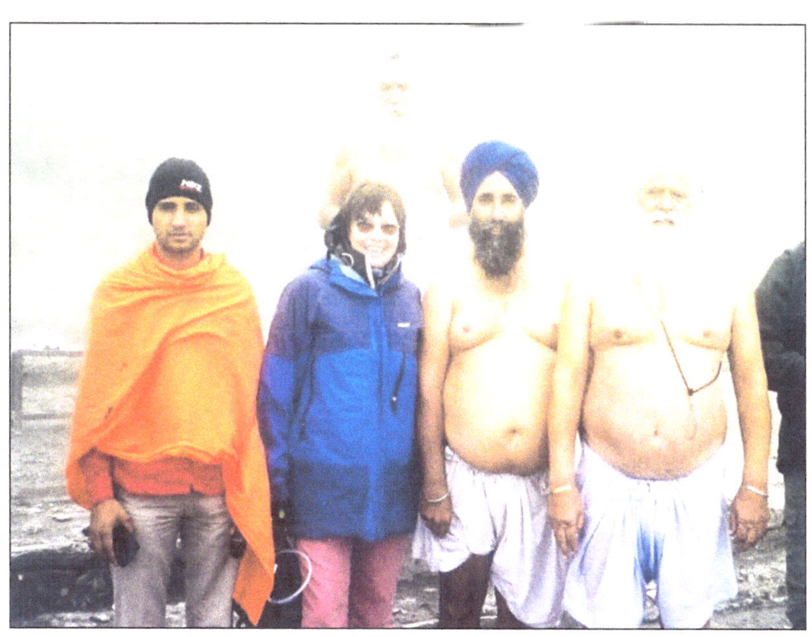

Scharlie makes friends

We go back and round the other way and cross a small wooden bridge over the stream. There is a bell above the bridge that people ring it as they cross and the sound merges with the sound of the horn from across the lake. We climb to look for flowers that Michael had told us about but there is no view, we are all tired and Scharlie is feeling cold, so we go back. We watch the men dipping in the lake. They strip down to their undershorts and black topknot and go right under the water. The young boys, here for the first time, are more reluctant than the fat old man. Two young brothers dunk under three times holding onto a chain fixed to the concrete side of the pool, encouraged by their mother then leap out and she hands them a towel.

We decide to set off down. Steve went on ahead and looking back saw Scharlie way above him walking her pony. She shouted for him to stop; she was tired and dizzy with the altitude and a passing pilgrim has told her to lengthen her stirrups so she can brace her legs. This probably saves her having an accident.

Steve chatted with the pilgrims, many of whom wanted to know where he was from. Many were from Bombay and all were most friendly and inquisitive. Steve took all the shortcuts, often being told he was going wrong. He came

Steve and Michael chat to one of the Hemkund cooks over a hot milky tea

upon a party he'd met earlier and they asked him if he had water. He wasn't sure if they were offering him some but realised something was wrong when the girl repeated, do you have water Stephen? Their grandmother was sitting slumped on the path and she needed water to take some pills. Steve took his water bottle out of his sac and told them it had lemon in it. He asked what was wrong and they said that she had fallen from her horse and had banged her head. He could see she had a big lump in the centre of her forehead.

Towards the bottom with Ghangaria well in view Steve came upon a road gang remaking the path. He watched them building an outer retaining wall of dry stone, which they top with cement to reduce frost damage. Then they lay flat stones for the road surface. The foreman asked if Steve was with party from UNESCO. The Forest Department officer had told the gang that we were from UNESCO, as he wanted to ginger everyone up. The foreman explained that he was contracted to repair the path and had hired Nepali workman to do the work. He pointed to the shantytown of blue plastic at the top end of the village and said that the Forest Department wouldn't let them build decent accommodation. He wanted me to ask for permission to build some shacks. He said the government wants the development and that

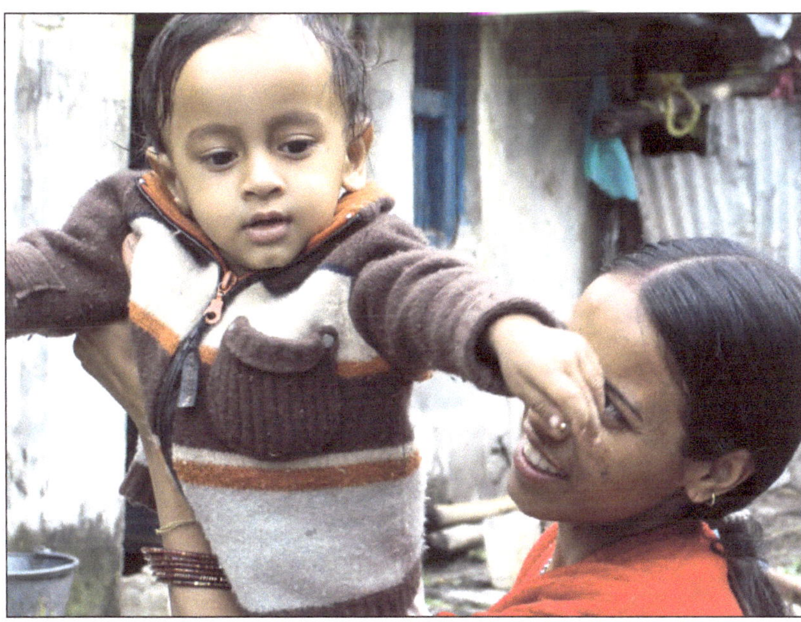

Young mother and toddler

workers would always be needed to repair and sweep and that they should have somewhere decent to live. Steve said he wasn't with UNESCO but that he would be seeing the forest officer later that evening and would raise the matter with him. The foreman seemed satisfied and Steve said goodbye and pressed on. Michael caught him up as he entered the village and they walked together. Steve told him about the road menders' complaints. Michael said that the Forest Department wouldn't want any more dwellings.

Scharlie said she felt really ill with the altitude. She was feeling more and more lightheaded and had entirely lost her appetite and had a bad headache. Altitude had really kicked in. When we reached the tent she took some pills and lay horizontal but the pain didn't go away. Everything felt distant and if she sat up she felt dizzy so she stayed still and refused supper. We had come up quickly and our campsite was just under 10,000 feet and Helmkund was at 4,084 m. Riding may have aggravated the problem because had she walked she might have been forced to turn back before getting so high. Steve got her into bed and brought her a drink and some paracetamol. You will be all right, its altitude, you'll soon acclimatise, just drift off to sleep, he encouraged.

There was to be a film about the Valley of Flowers at the visitor centre

Road gang making the path to Hemkund

Some of the elderly pilgrims are carried in makeshift sedan chairs

Others ride mules

that Michael said would be good. We were welcomed by three of four young women, and there were introductions and a speech about the Valley project from the head of the village. With government funding and support from the Forestry Department they had begun to manage the huge numbers of visitors that the Bhyundir Valley gets each summer. He said that they wanted to expand the winter tourism and would create facilities to cater for eco-tourists coming when there was snow in the valley. We were served tea and biscuits and chips fried in mild pepper that coloured them red. Michael said that they had done a good job in collecting the rubbish and in regulating the teashops, but now they needed to reduce the rubbish at source through a campaign to educate people. The Gundwara is doing its part to suggest that the whole pilgrimage is holy and shouldn't be fouled with litter. You never know, but seeds that are planted here in the Valley might bear fruit when people got back home. After all this is the home of the world famous Chipko movement, when women opposed the logging companies by tying themselves to the trees.

Steve managed to have a quiet word with Mr Bister about accommodation for the road menders. The Department wouldn't allow any shacks; they would be rented or sold and the problem will continue, he said. And anyway the people were only temporary. Steve wondered why the forest department did not constructs barrack-like dormitories. Mr Bister thought a moment and said it would be very expensive and the government would have to pay.

We watch the film about the clean up of the valley and the impact on the flora in the Valley of Flowers. Mr Bister's predecessor explained how you used to have to hold your nose while walking the pilgrim way because 10 to 20 yards either side of the path was full of rubbish and plastic bottles. He demonstrated that now you couldn't find even a matchstick. The flowers were shown with their medicinal properties, which were most extensive. Scharlie was still very ill when we got back but she managed to drink water and ate a couple of bowls of tomato soup. She has visions of having to be evacuated and spoiling the holiday. In the morning she says I don't think I can stand. But Steve doesn't give up. He says he will stay with her today and look after her and they 'll take it easy. She makes it to breakfast and forces down some cornflakes and hot milk.

Valley of the Flowers

Saturday 9 September

Today we go to the Valley of Flowers. The valley forms part of the Nanda Devi National Park or Bioshere Reserve and is known internationally for its meadows of endemic alpine flowers. It came to the attention of people in the West when British mountaineers Frank Smythe and Eric Shipton lost their way after climbing Mt Kamet and happened on the valley in 1931 and wrote about it on their return. (The upper Nanda Devi Sanctuary was reached by mountaineers Eric Shipton and Bill Tilman in 1934 having ascended the Rishi Ganga Gorge and Nanda Devi was climbed by Odell and Tilman in 1936.) Michael lived in the valley while doing his doctoral research on the rare musk deer and had always wanted to return. The valley is also home to other rare and endangered species including the Himalayan black bear, the goat-like goral and thar and the bharal or blue sheep. There have also been sightings of brown bear and snow leopard in the national park.

Michael and Steve begin the climb to the Valley of Flowers

Gorge at the entrance to the Valley of Flowers (photo Michael Green)

Valley of Flowers and Rataban 6166m (photo Michael Green)

Scharlie is still very ill, but Steve persuades her to drink something and she gradually gets herself ready. The main party leaves. It's a nice day. We are slow going through the village and stop at the bridge for a drink. We wonder if we'll catch the others up, but they are waiting for us at the entrance to the park where there is a Forest Department checkpoint. The path climbs up through a forest of huge pine. It is beautiful and we welcome the shade and go slowly at the back of the group. Slowly Scharlie begins to feel better and her head clears.

The trail drops to a bridge across the river and then climbs again. It's hot now that we are out of the forest and we fall behind. We lose the way at a landslide and have to clamber up to the path. A young man from our Sherpas has waited for us. He's squatting on a rock looking intently at a point on the landslip. We wait a couple of minutes and out pops a delightful marmot like creature about the size of a hamster that we learn later is called a Himalayan mouse.

We finally reached the opening into the Valley of Flowers and cross a metal bridge. There is little shade in the open meadow, the sun takes its toll and Scharlie limps along. Phil stops to paint at a large rock and we go on another

Sanjay and young sherpa on the rickety tin bridge

half a mile and to where the others have stopped for lunch. There is one small willow bush and a haven of soft green grass and Scharlie dives for the shade. She drinks her carton of juice and eats an apple but can't manage any of the rest of the ample packed lunch. She curls up and eventually sleeps or at least falls into a sort of restful stupor for three hours. Steve and Sanjay chat about mountaineering. Scharlie wakes, she's feeling better for the rest, and we set off back. The others catch up and pass us. When we get to the village we go to the visitor centre so Scharlie can watch the film from last night. It's freezing cold in the concrete auditorium and by the time the film has finished we are shivering. We go for finger chips and tea at the hotel before going back to the campsite for dinner.

Sanjay says he's getting married in December and produces a photograph of his bride to be. It is an arranged marriage, he says, and he makes us laugh with stories of how his family chose a wife. This is my last chance, he says. Michael makes jungle juice from limes and whiskey. Sanjay accepts a glass although he says he is teetotal. He gulps it down and says he can feel it moving all the way down his alimentary canal.

We rest for three hours while Scharlie sleeps under the shade of a willow

Sunday 10 September

Last night was blissful for Scharlie who managed to get comfortable and slept most of the night; happy at the thought that she has chosen to have a rest day. Steve brings her cornflakes and hot milk in bed. The others are going back to the Valley of Flowers to explore. Michael wants to go to Kunth Khal, a hanging valley above and to the west of the Valley of Flowers that was closed to trekkers in 1970 and has recently been opened again. Michael had wanted us to camp up there having got permission from the Forest Department. The idea is that we can each go as far and as fast as we want and that there will be sufficient young men to turn back whenever we want. Just after the bridge at the entrance to the Valley of Flowers we strike off to the left through thick foliage and cross a stream. A young man gives Steve a helping hand across the torrent and the team of young men energetically build a causeway for the others.

Sanjay has sent the lads ahead with an ice axe, ropes carabiners and jumars. But instead of climbing the gully as Sanjay anticipated, we climb up the right-hand side of the gully. There is a sort of a track through dense herbage but

Young sherpas help us across a torrent

Beginning the climb to the col on the Kunthkhal-Hanuman Chatti trek route

it's steep and the steps are unstable. Still we get up, three lads, plus a young man from the Forestry Department sent by Mr Bister to look after us. Jim and Phil have fallen back and one of the lads stayed with them. We reach a level area and contour along as the path has given out. I can see a ford across the stream below and a vague path beyond it. I point this out to our young leader but he ignores me and carries on thrashing up the hillside through the dense brush. I tell Michael I'll go down and look. I traverse around the rocks and then slide down through the undergrowth to the stream. There is a good ford with stones. The others follow and we stop for lunch. I go down to the stream to wash my face and eat my lunch there. The beach by the side of the stream seems to offer much easier walking than the dense vegetation on the raised banks. I try to point this out to our young guide but he crashes into the vegetation again, so I think I'll go it alone and set off along the beach. It narrows and I slip on a rock and wet my feet. The beach opens up again and I realise that I'm probably ahead of the others; I can't see them because they are lost in the undergrowth. After an hour I reach a high point where I can look back and see them far behind. There is a large rock on the skyline and I climb to it, take off my rucksack, have a drink and lie down. I can see the head wall of the

Start of the Kunthkhal path Valley of Flowers

valley less than a mile away and the col over to Hanuman Chatti. The terrain is bolder moraine but there are flowers and I can hear the call of a Monal bird.

The guides and the young forestry officer arrive and Michael and I walk on a ways to another rock and sit for an hour or so chatting. We scan the slopes with binoculars looking for blue sheep but all we see are black chough. I ask about Michael's work and the time he spent living here researching musk deer. He tells me that musk, weight for weight, is the most valuable animal product. It takes the glands from 40 males to produce a kilo, which currently sells for $45,000. The deer are solitary and holed up in the rhododendron forest during the day and come out in the open at night. They don't go down the mountain in winter, as most people suppose, but subsist on the rhododendron leaves. Michael had 150 sightings in the three years he lived here and many of these were with a night scope. We decide to head back and go back down the gully. It is pleasant walking back and we carry on chatting. I'm tired but feeling good; I've enjoyed stretching my legs and going fast on my own.

Back at the camp, after washing her hair under the ice-cold tap, Scharlie wandered down to the river and scrambled through yew and rhododendron

Himalayan Musk Deer (Moschus leucogaster) largely nocturnal (photo Siddharth Kaushik)

forest onto the flat rocky bank. The flowers here are perfectly balanced – perfect and peaceful. She felt completely safe, although there are black bears in the region and two were seen yesterday drinking on the other side of the river. The Sikhs believe that they come out of the forest and ravage young women.

We get back to the village and over dinner tell stories from the day and find out that Jess has had a narrow escape. She slipped on the way down and had to cling to a rock until the lad who was with her could reach down and hold her while she regained her footing. It pours in the night. We have been lucky with the weather so far – three fine days while we've been walking.

We squeeze into the cook tent and recount stories over the evening meal

Joshimath

Monday 11 September

It's still raining hard and Steve packs the gear in the tent and by the time he has finished, the rain has stopped. Phil is feeling ill with the altitude sickness and an upset stomach, and their tent leaked so they had an uncomfortable night. We catch them up and Steve decides to stay with them to road at Govindghat.

Scharlie is feeling much better so she goes on with Michael. It is hot and exhausting and she had forgotten how far we'd come; it seems longer between the tea houses than on the way up. She talks about her childhood in Jamaica and Michael says his father was in the military police and they lived in Kenya when Jomo Kenyatta was President at the end of the MauMau uprising and then in Cyprus when there was Eoca terrorism. The main part of the walk goes in and out of woodland but for the last hour it is in bright sunshine. Scharlie's clothes are wringing wet and she longs for the water Steve is carrying but she feels strong enough to reach the ancient bridge where the path plunges into the shade of the Aladdin's cave of shops.

Scharlie in Joshimath; Jim, reading The Times of India

Sanjay takes us to the rest house where Mr Bister lives. There is a loo, a cool restaurant where we can eat our packed lunch and somewhere to wash and change before we have to set off in the Jeeps. We wandered back into the bazaar to take photos before we leave. It's thronging with people and ponies and is the main street through the village, very narrow, with plastic and canvas stretched between the houses to form a coloured roof. We drive back down the gorge to Joshimath. We had almost forgotten the twisting road scarred by landslides and under continual repair. It's dug deep into the mountainside with huge overhanging rocks and the drop to the river is more or less sheer. Large white tourist buses pass us bearing pilgrims to the beginning of their journey. Now we have seen Helmkund ourselves we admire the elderly starting the long ascent.

Back at the guest house there is hot water and its bliss to wash. Scharlie is feeling better but is concerned about going back up to altitude. The mountains, where we are going next, are wreathed in clouds and look jagged and enormous from the guest house. Still two nights ago she thought she would have to abandon the whole trip.

Steve relaxing back at the Adventure Trekking base 'camp camp' in Josihmath

Lata

Tuesday 12 September

Scharlie stayed behind with Mary while the rest of us go to Joshimath to get a ski lift to a resort where you can get a good view of Nanda Devi and the big mountains. Scharlie lies in blessed peace and solitude that she doesn't want to end. Lime green walls, white ceiling with a mahogany brown fan, not on because a cool breeze streams in through the diamond grating of the casement window. The bed is firm with a comforting fluffy bedspread in lurid pink, orange and green. She could stay here quite happily for days. Her tummy is delicate, her noses is runny, her hips are sore from yesterday's walk and she feels in no condition to head into the mountains for a trek at high altitude.

Because Sanjay has to buy supplies, we don't get to the lift till nearly midday. There is a long queue so we decide not to bother and spend an hour or so telephoning and sending postcards from the post office. You need to get the stamps franked or you risk getting them steamed off, we are told. We

The children of Lata come out to greet us and have their photo taken

have lunch and finally set off after three. A quick lunch and away. Steve is still suffering from an overdose of petrol spilled in the back of his Jeep. The drive east towards Nanda Devi our next objective is unexpectedly beautiful, contouring along the side of a fertile terraced valley at about the same altitude as Joshimath. There are none of the straight ordered lines you see in Europe, and the different coloured fields follow the rocky contours. There have been landslides and the cliffs above us are unstable. At one point we are held up while a bulldozer clears a way.

We arrive at a hamlet to a commotion of welcome from the villagers, many of whom are hoping to be our porters. The children – separate groups of boys and girls, giggle and pull away when we take photos, then shyly come to see themselves on the digital cameras. Two tykes on their own may have come from the Untouchables village. While the porters are loading up, the children rush over to where a young woman distributes large cardboard boxes labelled, 'World Food Aid – Biscuits from Italy'. It seems that each child is given a small pack of biscuits each day if they come to school. We start off at a track accompanied by two forestry officers and the children with their

Children carrying World Aid biscuits to their school in Lata

boxes. There are black clouds bubbling up the valley from the west and it begins to rain as we reach the schoolhouse where we are to spend the night. The children entertain us to floorshow of Indian dancing while Sanjay cooks. Then the children play statues running about madly then freezing in martial art poses – girls and boys are playing together now. They sing Old Macdonald's Farm in Hindi. Jess distributes pens and they crowd round her to write their names. Then two little girls offer to dance for us. They're very accomplished, singing in a high whining way, while their bodies move sinuously, arms and hands creating intricate patterns. The children watch them with delight and one little girl tries to copy.

We are at a home-stay in the village tonight and don't know what to expect. It grows cold and we get the duvet jacket out for Scharlie. At about 7.30 Sanjay brings tea and biscuits and we sit in a circle around the gas lamp and candle. The candle splutters in the breeze and finally goes out. After dinner the Sherpas clear away and help us carry our belongings over to the village. We have both stiffened from sitting in the cold and we hold onto each other down the slippery path.

The village is delightful. Traditional houses with stone roofs and colourful

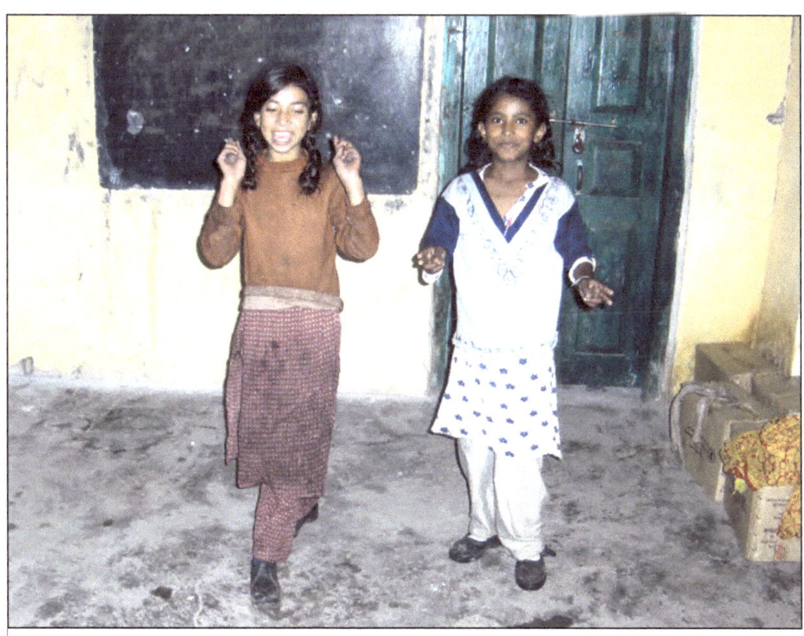

Two girls dance, singing in a high pitch, their hands and bodies making intricate patterns

wooden balconies cling to the steep hillside. We drop off one by one at different guest houses and pass the square where there will be dancing later. Two young boys are practising their drumbeat round the campfire.

We are at the back of the file so get the last house. It's a small square room and the floor bounces as you walk on it. There are two beds, one big enough for us both, each with bright covers. There is electric light and candles and it's all very cheery and warm. The ceiling is made from wide sawn planks and the walls are lime washed plaster over rough stone. There is an Indian loo a few yards away up the hill, which we share with four or five other houses around us. The beds are hard, just a blanket over boards, so we get out the mattresses and roll out the sleeping bags. We had thought we'd be sleeping in the open covered porch of the school, so it's a pleasant surprise to be so well catered for. Sanjay is in two minds about our stay here. He keeps making comments that this isn't his area, he is from Joshimath and he isn't sure about here. In this valley the women do all the work and the men sit around and drink, he says.

A dance is due to begin in the village square in the centre of the village and we go and see what's happening. Five old women and three old men are shuffling around singing a dirge as they face each other in pairs, holding each

Our snug home stay with its candles. hard plank bed and white washed walls

other's arms. People are gathered in family groups and it seems as if they sit in the corner of the square nearest to where they live. Women sit together wearing brightly coloured scarves. They chat animatedly and take very little notice of others. There are many more women than men, and a lot of children. We are sitting next to a group of women near our end of the village. It is convivial and everyone is in good humour. The dance seems to pantomime planting and reaping of crops and we think they are scattering seeds. Sanjay tries to explain the story and we gather that they are sowing corn when the devil tries to take away one of their children. A father promises to let the devil come back later and take the child but he breaks his promise.

Two lads then take the drums that have been warming in front of the fire in the centre of the square. One of the small boys is good at beating out the rhythm with two sticks on a conical drum. The older boy hit the base note with his hand at one end and a stick at the other. A young man seemed to be administering to the leader of the dance – bringing him a crucible full of coals from the fire that the old man swung around as he danced.

Three young men join in the dance, which seems to be a slow conga, the three old men taking the lead, bobbing and weaving like exotic birds. The old

Dance in the village square telling a story about the devil kidnapping a young boy

men are lithe and wiry. There was a quiet interlude with just the old people dancing like they had at the beginning and the drums were put back in front of the fire to warm. Older men take over the drums from the boys and more people joined the dance. We notice the headman of the village burning incense or some drug in a shrine that the male dancers keep retreating to. The old people look spaced out, but maybe that is the rhythm of the drums. The beat gets faster and more people join in. A rather distinguished woman, sitting near the stage, acknowledges the dancers by putting her hands together in prayer and a man and woman perform some strange ritual with a ball of thread, passing it back and forth to make a rope and then unravelling it all and rolling it up again. The final act is quite dramatic. Having circled the fire in a conga, each of the dancers put their heads on the base drum as it is beaten then collapses and is helped to the side and we are unsure if the devil or the villagers have won. Finally the dancer, who is maybe playing the devil, collapses and everyone gets up and files off home and it is all over. We made our way back to our room in the dark, taking care not to slip on the muddy stone steps.

Lata in the morning, mother of vilage head man examining us from her balcony

Wednesday 13 September

The village in the morning light is delightful. The houses have stone rooms and blue wooden balconies. Each house is surrounded by vegetable garden and there are neat stacks of firewood everywhere. We learn that the village has a stretch of communal forest. We stop for breakfast in front of the house belong to the head porter. An old lady, his mother maybe, comes out on to the balcony to see these strange folk. We are brought a pail of hot water to wash. There are new potatoes from the garden for breakfast along with the usual porridge and a heavy green chapatti made from flour from the red plant we see growing on all the terraces below the village.

The group gathers and we go up the hill to pay our respects to the Goddess Nanda in the village shrine. It's a beautiful temple of brownstone and we take off our shoes to enter the courtyard. There is a bell to ring before entering the inner sanctum and a young man puts a red mark on our foreheads. We cross over to the school and about 40 small children are lined up doing drill. There is a small boy in charge taking them through the parts of the body. He shouts out the name in English and the children point to the part on their own bodies

We pay our repects at the Buddist temple above the village

Children in Lata school

Courtyard of our homestay in Lata

Traditional house in Lata

Woman preparing our breakfast of potato and green chapatti

and repeat the word. It is very rhythmic and they obviously enjoy it. Then they divide into two groups – one lot crushing into the tiny classroom to be taught by one of the 12-year-olds, the others remaining on the porch. They sit on a long mat on the floor. The teacher will come from Joshimath later and stay for two hours. So the monitor system seems to be working. We take pictures and laugh with the children and generally disrupt the classes.

Finally we set off to Lata Karack on a beautifully made forest path. Some way above the village we find a large group of people clearing rocks and vegetation to make a campsite. They are making camp for a party from Bombay who we meet a little higher up. They tell us that they have been trekking in Garhwal and seem well off and speak good English.

We climb slowly but Scharlie begins to feel the altitude and Steve stays with her. It is a lovely path rising through pinewoods. The trees begin to thin out and the path climbs through shrubs and flowers – gentians, asters, phlomis, geraniums and lots of herbs. It is a gorgeous afternoon and it gets colder as we go up so we don't mind the hot sun. We zigzag around a rocky bluff and reach a shady spot for lunch but don't stop long because it's another 1,500 feet. The

We begin the ascent to Lata Karack

last stretch is a killer and about 500 feet below the hut Scharlie really begins to feel the altitude and staggers in breathing heavily. It takes her 15 minutes just to change into warm clothes because her socks stick to the Velcro of her sandals and she is too weak to pull them apart.

There are four rooms in the hutment and a long veranda. The site is spectacularly beautiful, but there is no view as the faraway mountains are covered in cloud. We have dinner and Michael asks where we'd like to sleep. The others opt to sleep on the floor in the wooden hut but we choose a tent because it seems quieter. Steve carries the gear down and lays out the mats and sleeping bags. Hot soup is most welcome now the sun has gone and it's getting cold. Steve helps Scharlie down the steep slope and we get snugged up and in the event have a good night.

Scharlie makes it to the huts at Lata Karack despite feeling desperately ill with altitude

Nanda Devi

Thursday 14 September

It is a nice day and we wake early and get a great view of the mountains, high and white through the trees. We pack and Sanjay brings us tea, then we make our laboured way up to the hut for breakfast of porridge. The path today curves gently across grassy fells like walking in the Lake District. We contour up the hillside and keep climbing to the Dharansi Pass at 4,000 m. The path zigzags and we climb a knoll where the Americans are camped and contour around the mountain on a level path. The local stone splits naturally into slabs about 2 inches thick and the path has been built like a gigantic National Trust scheme with virtually no scrambling necessary except on one or two steep bits over rock buttresses where the unobtrusive khaki presence of the forest officer is on hand to make sure his charges are safe. He regularly fishes out his radio telephone to report to headquarters. But little scrambles are not a problem for us and Scharlie is keeping up today.

View of Hathi Parbat (Elephant Peak) 6,727m from Lata Karack (photo Michael Green)

Sanjay wakes us with tea in bed (photo Michael Green)

We begin the spectacular traverse above the Rishi Ganga gorge (photo Michael Green)

There has been a dispute with porters. Sanjay is upset and says he always has this trouble with people from Lata since the village has a monopoly on porters for Nanda Devi and they insist he take more porters than he needs. We could hear the row brewing this morning at Lata Karack and it seems he may have dismissed some of them. The head porter, Ragbir Singh, seems to carry more than anyone else, including a load of pots wrapped in cloth in his hands, but others seem lightly laden. At the lunch break, where the path to Tolma goes off to the left, Sanjay distributes some of his load to the others who have less.

After lunch we continue contouring and can see cloud poring over from the other side of the ridge and know we are near the pass. In Scharlie's mind the dangers of the traverse have attained mythic proportions. Michael had warned us about steep slopes and long drops and his description had conjured up something horrific in her imagination. She is expecting a knife-edge path carved from solid rock with a 1,000-foot sheer drop. She's not nervous because altitude sickness has taken her onto a new plane of determination and fortitude. In the event, however, the traverse turns out to be fine. The scrambly path is well made and contours round and there are no real cliffs. It

Traverse line to Dharansi Pass (photo Michael Green)

is a little like parts of the GR20 in Corsica, with views thousands of feet down to jagged pinnacles guarding the Rishi Ganga Gorge that Shipton and Tilman ascended to climb Nanda Devi. The grass-covered slopes below us are steep but there is plenty to grab onto should you trip. For extra safety Steve walks behind so he can grab Scharlie's rucksack if she stumbles. It's slightly downhill and Scharlie feels more energised than she has for days. We see lots of red potentilla and blue gentians and even some ranunculus and purple aconitium.

We climb a gully to get onto a higher traverse line to avoid a cliff and the path continues at a higher level until we round a corner and see a low stone arch and a view of the campsite. There is a long grass slope down and another half an hour brings us to the tents pitched on a pavement of slabs. It's foggy and cold and we dive into the same yellow tent we had last night and change into our warmest gear. Scharlie did well to make it, considering how unwell she is. It's very cold in the night and we are only just warm enough. Scharlie sleeps in all her clothes including her hat. It's clear and we can see the stars.

Campsite at Dharansi Pass (photo Michael Green)

Friday 15 September

Steve woke at 5.30, hair wet with condensation. He scrambled into his clothes and is out by 5.45, early enough to see the mountains as the sun rises. It is cold and there is ice on the tent and the rocks are slippy. Scharlie decides to have a few more minutes in bed and goes back to sleep. Steve heads off along the path towards the cairns on the skyline. It is very clear and around a corner there is a view of Nanda Devi herself. Bertholi, the mountain to the south we can see from the campsite, is in the sun and Dunagiri, the handmaiden of Nanda, and Changabang look beautiful in the morning light. Phil, Anna, Jess, and Jim arrive and we take photos and hang about enjoying the views. The sun comes up over Nanda Devi and it begins to warm but Steve hasn't put on enough clothes and after an hour or so he goes back to the tents to see if Scharlie is up and would like to walk over. Sanjay says breakfast is nearly ready. We swallow some not quite cooked hot gruel and set off. The sun is warm now. Perhaps the mountains are not so clear but the warmth is pleasant and we chat about the inner sanctuary and how long it would take to climb the Rishi Ganga Gorge. Nanda Devi isn't as clear, but it is not yet in cloud so Scharlie gets a good view.

Bethatoli Himal 6,352m from campsite (photo Michael Green)

Scharlie near Dharansi Pass

Chilly early morning with Nanda Devi

By the time we get back Michael and Jim are just setting off towards Dunagiri in search of Himalayan blue sheep, a rare goat like creature that is the favoured prey of snow leopard. They mount the ridge, Jim carrying his umbrella. Two Sherpas follow, instructed by Sanjay plus the forest officer, who, noticing their departure, quietly follows. Scharlie has decided to spend the day lying in her sleeping bag in the sun glad of the rest, but Steve packs a rucksack with spare clothes and water and follows them. It is tough going, fast uphill and he's breathing hard by the time he catches them up on the top of the first ridge. We traverse right until we can see into the basin below Nanda Devi and are rewarded by the sight of a flock of about 16 or 17 blue sheep. We keep low on the ridge. A pair of lammergeier circle in thermals above us, and then a third flies directly above us and then over the pass between Dunagiri and Nanda Devi. They are immensely impressive; effortlessly cruising around and covering the ground have been seen flying as high as 25,000 feet on Everest. They live almost exclusively on a diet of bones and young vultures have to learn how to carry bones weighing as much as themselves to a height of four or five hundred feet before dropping them onto rocks to crack them into smaller pieces and expose the marrow.

Himalayan Blue Sheep or Bharal - favoured prey of Snow Leopard (photo Sirsendu Gayen)

Walking back Steve comes across the young porters crawling into a cave in the boulder moraine above the camp to collect the ice we need for water. Having lived with the imperative to reach the tops of mountains it is discomfiting to be here looking at these amazing peaks and being unable to climb them. Of course it is completely unrealistic to even imagine climbing Nanda Devi, nevertheless Steve felt he had achieved something. After a big cooked lunch we have a sleep and get warm. It is a starry cloudless night and very cold in the night and we have to put more clothes on, including our fleece, to get warm enough to sleep.

Saturday 16 September

We have a leisurely start because it's very cold, there is thick ice on the tents and the rocks will be slippy with ice. There is a long gradual slope that contours up to the big cairn at the start of the traverse. Steve is in the lead and tries setting a slow even pace that will keep the group together; we don't want anyone rushing to catch up and slipping. We capture a last view of Nanda Devi. Scharlie found the uphill stretches on the traverse hard and Steve helped

Whole party at Dharansi Pass

by letting her pull on his stick. Her breathing is still fast and loud and her legs feel so weak. The only easy bit was the scramble down the scree. We reach the junction to Lata and stop for lunch. The Sherpas have so much excess energy they built huge extension to the existing cairn. The rock here contains lots of mica and the cairn looks like a silver labrador dog sitting up to beg. Sanjay had made extra eggs and chapattis for us because we had a long walk but a lot of it was left. The Sherpas were glad of it later as they were not offered any refreshment in Tolma. The path is much steeper than the way we came up; strange that the Indian group we met preferred this way. It is open country at first and then forest with huge cedar, birch and rowan. It's a long way down 5,000 feet to the village and the path zigzags across low growing shrubs like dwarf rhododendron then into woodland of birch and sorbus. The understory is made up of ferns, mosses and wild rose. Gnarled birch trees 50 feet high and with trunks 3 foot in diameter. Where trees have fallen, a foothold has been chopped to help you climb over or if there is room you duck under. We get water someone has laid leaves to direct the trickle of water down the stem of a leaf.

Michael and Steve stride ahead on the last thousand feet and reach the

Scharlie on our way back

One of the trickier sections of the traverse from Dharansi Pass

village about 4.20pm. For Scharlie, near the end, exhaustion was setting in and her legs were moving automatically in a trance. But she wasn't feeling ill from altitude and had no headache or sickness. Tolma is on a beautiful site on the south side of a steep gorge. There are marvellous views of steep green meadows, with isolated conifers and steep sandstone crags. The sun is still out when we arrive on the terrace of one of the homestays. We are welcomed and taken to a rooftop terrace for tea and fresh apples plucked from heavily laden trees nearby. Fodder and beans are drying on the flat roofs. In the courtyard below us women shake the beans out of pods, then carefully sweep the empty husks into a pile with grass brooms. The terraces are intensively farmed and it seems the village grows most of what it needs apart from rice. We are assigned our rooms. Our party is shown to three different home stays where we will eat our separate suppers. They are still fitting a solar panel as we arrive so Scharlie and I go back up to the main homestay while they finish the DIY.

We join a queue for the loo. The latrine is in an orchard about 100 yards away down concrete steps and down a broken stone path that will be hard

Micdael relaxes on a moss covered tree

to negotiate in the dark; we've been warned it's like being on an ice and everyone that falls over. Michael also says this village is visited at night by bears! So we go in great trepidation with the head torch. But just as we are waiting for a bucket of water a fairy light on a bit of cable comes on and we can at least see. We manage a good wash by pouring warm water from a jug over each other.

Sunday 17 September

Tea, potatoes and beans for breakfast. The Americans came and interviewed Michael. They are getting to grips with all the local infighting and understanding the benefits and drawbacks of the forestry department involvement in eco development. Scharlie takes a short walk down to the road while the drivers are loading the luggage. It is hot and she wanders down to the river and sits in the shade. A group of men are washing their clothes and themselves at the same time. They are dressed only in their loincloths and will dress in their wet clothes when they have finished bathing.

Phil and I are intrigued by the construction methods in the village. The older

Woman sorting fodder on her stone roof

traditional houses of wood and stone have balconies on each side supported on the projecting floor joists of the upper floor. They are semi-detached and a cupboard accessed from inside the house divides the balcony. The upper floor is reached by an external staircase.

The house where we are staying has been divided and one half is being demolished to make way for a concrete flat roofed dwelling with three homestay rooms. The brother of our host and his family have moved out to make room for us. The house next door, where the ceremony to make contact with the ancestors took place last night, is still intact. The family seem more old-fashioned or traditional than ours. This morning smoke is pouring out from under every stone roof slab and every hole in the structure as the women prepare breakfast. Our family cook on a kerosene stove.

The roadside village is totally different. They come down here for the three hardest winter months. But now it's like a frontier town in Venezuela – oil and dirt, unsavoury men and vehicles – lots of army trucks; this road was built after the Chinese threats to the border in 1969. We climb in the vehicles for the bumpy ride back to Joshimath. We have an hour, so walk the length of the main street looking at all the shops and kiosks. These people are so industrious. We

Bumpy road back to Joshimath (photo Michael Green)

see father and son making a bed. They are using a long wooden plane with handles at the front that the son pulls while the father guides. They see me watching and smile. There are men cutting steel angle to length with a hammer and chisel to make gates, a man welding an elaborate railing, men sitting in the road repairing shoes and sandals, and a man in kiosk making trousers on a treadle sewing machine. There are vegetable sellers and a goldsmith repairing an intricate gold necklace while women in saris watch in rapt attention on a bench in his tiny kiosk. There is a stall that repairs old kerosene stoves. The man and his stall are filthy, but he is providing a useful service. The sari fabric shops are the largest by far and are a favourite with the women – all the colours of the rainbow in traditional cotton or gaudy polyester. There is a shop selling shoes and women down from the villages, looking at pans and household gadgets.

We go up to Sanjay's house and Steve grabs a bedroom and collapses. We've done our turn camping and hope others don't feel aggrieved. We managed to get up to eat a little and congratulate Sanjay on a well-run trek. We've been listening to Anna washing and can hear her say her hands are dropping off. They won't have time to get their washing done in Delhi, so

Mary shopping

she needs to do it. We have lunch in a thali restaurant, where Sanjay gets a discount and meet Dr Singh, an Ayurvedic practitioner. He's charming and says he uses Western medicine for emergencies and herbs for everyday. He has a nursery where he is trying to grow rare medicinal plants. Scharlie and some of the others go to meet him later at his surgery. The taxi drops them next to a roadside statue of a bearded gentleman, like a large garden gnome who, it turns out, is the patron of medics. There is a small hut surrounded by fruit trees on a terrace and an old man greets them. He says that he used to be a patient, but now he looks after the garden. He knows little about the plants but keeps the place secure.

Dr Singh arrives with a botany student who identifies the plants and tells us the botanical names. Although rather weedy, the plants he has grown from seed and raised in the open ground seem healthy. The ones he has in clay pots are rather less so; the soil looks heavy and too wet. He asks advice and Scharlie and Jim suggest making a lighter compost. On the way back the student gives Scharlie his card and a letter of recommendation from his university and tells her it is his ambition to become a taxonomist and to work in the Himalayas. He says his dream is to come to England but it's not clear what Scharlie can do for him.

A final meal has been prepared and Santosh and Sanjay want feedback on the trek. Sanjay as usual has given his all. He is nostalgic and emotional. It is important that we give him a good report to his boss, Santosh. Without exception everyone in the group is complimentary. We say we admired his commitment, his patience and humour, and his organisation. He asks for suggestions and we can't think of anything except to suggest they might consider smaller lunch packs; you don't feel like eating a lot at lunchtime in high mountains and it seems a shame to waste food. Michael is touched when Sanjay says that we are the best group he has ever led and that we have been more like a family than clients. He is hoping that Santosh will build a house for him and his new wife now they work hand-in-hand for the company. His guru has told him that his fortunes are looking up, he says.

Monday 18 September

We manage some sleep but Steve is ill in the morning and has not finished packing when they want to load up. He rushes to finish. He's in a state – he's just pulled on a shirt and pants to have breakfast and hasn't managed to wash or find his underpants. He finally finds them under a chair, but puts them down and can't find them again. For some reason it upsets him mightily and he sits on a chair and wants to cry. But there's no time and Scharlie is too ill to help so he has to bung everything into a bag so that they can strap it on the roof of one of the vehicles. He checks the bags are strapped on properly and climbs aboard.

The eight-hour drive to Himalayan Hideaway is a nightmare. Scharlie has grabbed a back seat in the nearest vehicle and Michael, Bill and Anna join us. Fortunately it is the one driven by the tall man with gentle hands and quick reflexes. We try and get comfortable in the cramped space. It's very cold for the first part of the journey and Steve had packed his fleece thinking it would be hot. So he dragged a bit of Scharlie's fleece over himself and tried to sleep. By closing his eyes he can somehow reach a calm state of mind to deal with

We say goodbye to our Adventure Trek guides in Joshimath (photo Michael Green)

his awful head cold and the bumps and rigours of the road.

We stop for a drink and Steve stretches out on the backseat. Too soon we set off again. Steve changed to behind the driver because there's more room and manages to rest his head on the seat back and cram his hat over his eyes. Our world settles into a continuous blur of bumps and twists and shakes. Our drive delivers us to a pleasant airy restaurant for lunch; he knows all the good places. When we stop our heads spin as if we've been at sea. There's a huge ficus giving shade by the restaurant and Michael finds a Bo leaf from the tree the Buddha is said to have sat under. Everyone else seems fine and eats heartily but we are both feeling ill and have a plate of chips and lime juice.

The second half of the journey is even worse but there is nothing we can do but endure and know that every mile is bringing us closer to comfort. We sit up and watch the road to avoid getting carsick. We're intrigued by the road gangs. They live by the side of the road in makeshift shelters of corrugated iron or plastic sheeting. There are women with them and some children. The look clean and well dressed despite the poor conditions. We imagine they establish camp where they can get water. The job is arduous; nearly everything is done by hand. In some places there are teams with hardhats, compressors,

Road gang splittng slabs with a sledgehammer and wedge

drills and dynamite who are supervised by an army engineer and, where there has been a landslide, there might be a bulldozer and an army driver. In other places the men are working with shovels, sledgehammers and long chisels. The job is dangerous; the slopes they are working under are unstable. There are great hanging blocks of rocks, huge slanting slabs and tons of loose gravel and sandy earth. It is bad enough having to drive past it. But having to work directly under it all day must result in a lot of accidents. Do the men get any compensation? What do the women do if their men are injured? This must be the high season for road maintenance after the monsoon, but before the cold of winter; we can't see how they could endure the cold in their plastic shelters. What impresses us most is their fortitude. The men are organised and strong looking. The work, which at first sight seems chaotic, is in fact methodical and systematic. And the women manage to maintain some sort of home in the most insecure and squalid conditions. In this section of the road the men are laying conduit – one green one and one orange. They're digging the trench by hand – breaking huge boulders with hammer and chisel. It seems so inefficient. Yet India has lots of labour. The cost of living is so much lower here because

Mary shopping

lots of people want work. So an item, like a battery for a camera, a meal in the restaurant, a bus fare, all cost a tenth of what they do back home. How can a manufactured item like a battery be so much less here? It must be all the people that are involved in getting that product into the customer's hands are paid so much less here. So it is the supply of labour that sets both the wage rate and the price of goods and therefore the cost of living.

We stop for one last time at a restaurant with a shaded garden. The loos are a walk up the hill through a garden. Not a huge challenge after what we've been doing; but limbs are stiff and tired. We are in rafting country and on the other side of the road we can watch the Ganges flow past filled with post monsoon rain. Phil does the calculations. We can walk at 2 m/s and the water is flowing at least twice as fast. The river is so wide and might be so deep, therefore so many cubic metres per second. It sounds a lot. Then he calculates how much potential energy that is and how much electricity it would generate. The answer is in gigawatts. We have a drink and set off for the final leg.

A brief hold-up with another landslide and we finally arrived at Himalayan Hideaway. It seems even more comfortable and attractive than it did two weeks ago on our way up into the mountains. Our bags are dusty from sitting on the top of the vehicle so Steve pops them in the shower. Blessed quiet and freedom from the motion as we lie on the bed in the cool interior and we get a couple of hours rest before dinner in the garden. Michael and Mary have asked for a barbecue and we sit in a semicircle around the circular brick-lined fire pit eating popcorn, grilled chicken and cheese. It is very pleasant but Steve's ears are blocked and he can't hear anything. The seating arrangement doesn't help conversation and we attempt to move the heavy iron seating around. The waiters bring us beer with roasted chicken and cheese and salad in a spicy dressing. We eat our fill. Then we are invited to the dining room for the main meal! There is a bean and tomato salad and scalloped potato.

Mussoorie

Tuesday 19 September

Today we part company. We are off to Mussoorie with. Anna, Phil, Jess and Ali are going back to Haridwar to take the train to Delhi. Michael and Mary meanwhile have arranged a blast from the past and over breakfast it arrives in the form of a Royal Enfield Bullet motorcycle. Michael rode one of these when he was living here nearly 30 years ago and the two met when he gave her a lift on his motorbike. The forest department has arranged the hire of a motorbike and a man called Lucky delivers it. Michael goes for a spin to refresh his road skills. We all gather to see them depart. There are no panniers so they have to downsize their luggage to Mary's green rucksack. They try on the helmets; they don't fit very well. We can see they are nervous and excited at the prospect. They climb aboard and with a throaty roar they are off, up over the mountain route to Mussoorie. We climb into our vehicle and set off too. It is much less crowded with just three people, but our driver has an unusual

Musoorie, hill station town NW of Dehra Dun

alarming hard on accelerator and brake driving style. He hauls on the wheel as if he is steering a large sailing ship and leans into the bends in an effort to drag it round. Maybe the steering is so awful this is the only way to steer. He's also very heavy with the horn, brake and accelerator and despite our relatively low power, wants to overtake everything in front. We go through Rishikesh and are glad we are not spending the day there with the others.

We are driving along the edge of a big National Park. There is dense jungle on either side. We are in the Siwalik Hills. The air immediately cools and we can imagine tigers stalking amongst the stately trees. Termite mounds a few feet high rise like fairy castles on the forest floor. It is cold in the forest and there are lots of monkeys near the road and Scharlie wants to stop and take photographs, but our driver ignores her, perhaps not understanding her desire to photograph a monkey. He is on a mission. He was contracted to take us to Dehra Dun, but we have negotiated for him to take us to Mussoorie, an extra three hours journey and he has to drive all the way back to Joshimath and will not get back till midnight.

He gets a bit lost in Dehra Dun. There are very few road signs and he

Mary and Michael set off on their nostalgic Royal Enfield motorcycle adventure

has to keep stopping to ask directions. There are lots of children and young people coming home from school or college. The town seems to be an educational centre. Finally we get back onto the main road and start the climb to Mussoorie. The road is better than anything we have been on – a deep metalled surface, with no sign of landslip, well-made stone revetments and solid concrete barriers. It may date from the Raj for all we know. But Mussoorie is a pale shadow of its glory days – crumbling colonial buildings fester on every side. We get to the car park and our driver wants to leave us here, but we are nowhere near our hotel. He says there is no parking further on but we persuade him to go a little further. We reach the gate at the end of the pedestrianised mall and our driver organises two rickshaws for us. We pay him and give him a tip. He seems pleased. Our rickshaw drivers struggle with our baggage but it is not far to the hotel. The Mall is a little like an English seaside promenade but full of rickshaws, honking scooters and motorbikes, people selling clothes, monkeys and the occasional cow.

Two men carry our bags and wait while we clarify if they have rooms for us. We asked them how much. They look at each other and say 100. We

Jim and Scharlie outside our hotel, the Padmini Nivas

know it's too much but give them 50 each. They smile. Our hotel, the Padmini Nivas, is an elegant rambling structure with a green corrugated roof and wide verandas. The plan is an arch overlooking the valley with windows all round. The guidebook mentions a well-stocked nursery of ornamental plants but little sign remains of its former glory. Likewise the games room, a padlocked conservatory, where the table tennis table and pool table look as though they have not seen a game for many a year. The general impression is grimy and rundown, but we're tired and decide to stay.

We are shown a suite and two smaller rooms. Jim isn't pleased with his room. It's too filthy to sleep in, he says and you can't walk barefoot on the carpet for fear of getting stuck in the gunge. But it's cheap. We sign in, get the keys and have a rest before venturing out for lunch on the Mall at a nice restaurant serving southern Indian vegetarian food. It seems to be a pattern. The restaurant we went to in Delhi also served the same food but the restaurant here looks cleaner and more appetising. We wander down The Mall, do some window-shopping and have lunch in a nice restaurant. We go back to the hotel, and while Scharlie rests Steve goes off exploring.

Manager Padmini Nives Hotel

Steve goes down to reception to get directions from the manager. On the desk he notices some small square black and white paintings showing stick-like figures. The manager puts them away in brown paper. There is a brush and tiny pot of paint and Steve asks about them. He says you have to keep busy. He takes the paintings out of their wrapping. They are very detailed and seem to be telling a story. The manager says it is tribal art that he learnt from the Warli people. Warli used to be forest people living in the jungle, but had been displaced by development and when the manager met them after finishing his studies in Bombay they were living by the side of the road, the men working as day labourers and the women painted on bark with rice paint. The paintings are like aboriginal paintings in that they tell a story in pictograms. The women still did the paintings for weddings and national festivals and when asked, they said they did them because their fathers had done them. But they no longer kept to the ceremonies and beliefs of their forest religion and had adopted Hindu festivals and images from the modern technological world. The paintings are recurring themes of rustic houses, palm trees and lines of ant-like people, painted with two triangles forming the body and stick like arms and legs. He says the two triangles represent the Yonhi and the Lingum, the male

Warli painting

and female. In all living forms these two triangles come together to make life. The dots are energy. Everything is energy – water, earth, sky and everything in between. In the centre of the painting there is a God riding an animal or bird. He says that the creature provides character – a tiger for strength or a peacock for beauty.

Back in our room the bed linen looks crumpled, the room is damp and musty and the whole hotel needs a makeover. Scharlie is planning a rest while Steve is out. She draws back the bedclothes and finds a large spider nestling behind the pillow. It's 5 inches across with a pale transparent body and visible fangs. She evicts it and gets into bed. Later we find its partner in the cupboard.

Steve has a map showing the National rail booking office and tourist office. The National rail office is derelict but a man in a nearby store assures him it will open tomorrow morning. Steve is also looking out for a suitable hotel; our hotel is fully booked on our last night. The nicest hotel is the Horizon the far end of the mall, just beyond the gate. It is clean and modern and convenient for the taxi when we leave on Friday. The receptionist, a thin face man with a dark moustache and oriental eyes, does us a deal for two rooms. On the way back Steve also visits the Kasmanda Palace, which we have been

Natinal rail booking office

recommended. He's shown the Royal bedrooms, which are very splendid. The main stairway has tiger skins, stuffed rhino and photos of distinguished Indians. The manager explains that until recently this was the summer residence of the Prince of Kasmanda, near Lucknow and that the hotel is still owned by the family and has recently been renovated. Unlike all the other old buildings in Mussoorie this is the only one in decent condition. Steve also finds the Rice Boat, a Tibetan restaurant that looks nice.

Wednesday 20 September

We decide to walk to the Buddhist temple. It is a long walk, but pleasant and cool under overhanging trees. Like the Mall there is a lot of cast-iron railing and lighting dating from the time of the Raj. We meander out of town watching the kites wheeling below us where the road verge drops into the jungle. We have not gone a mile when Michael and Mary come riding towards us looking happy and carefree on their motorbike. They are in flip-flops and without helmets today. They had wondered whether they might see us. They are off shopping and Michael asked if we want to take the motorbike for a spin. Jim

We visit the Buddist Temple in Mussoorie

has first go while Scharlie and I continue walking. Jim says it's always been his ambition to ride a bike in India and he gets Steve to take his photo. After he had got the hang of it, he gives Scharlie a lift to the Buddhist temple. Then it was Steve's turn. The bike looked and sounded the part, but once aboard there were some serious flaws. The gear change was like stirring porridge with a large spoon and the brakes were spongy and weak. He nearly came to grief when, unable to brake quickly enough, he had to jink past a parked vehicle and an oncoming taxi. He made it back, but his hips were sore and he could hardly walk. He had been in pain the whole trek and discovered back in England that he needed a new hip.

We sat for a while contemplating the temple, watching an old monk busy himself watering the plants. We removed our shoes and had a look round. It is highly chromatic with tromp d'oeil freezes and gaudy colours, but light and pleasant with windows on both sides. There is image of the Buddha in the centre and a life-size photo of the Dalai Lama. Jim shows us how to turn the prayer wheels. The larger ones are surprisingly heavy. Two Tibetan ladies followed Steve as he turned the wheels, praying Ome Padme Hum as they

Michael is much more relaxed on the motorbike now - no helmet and flip-flops

went and touching the final post with their foreheads.

We arranged to have lunch with Michael and Mary at their hotel, the Carlton's Plaisance. We waited for them in the garden and watched two grey-haired Anglo-Indian sisters climb into a chauffeured car. They might have been the owners. The hotel is a little like the Kasmanda Palace, only better preserved and more of a family home. They show us their bedroom, which was a suite with an enclosed terrace where they had breakfast. It's large and full of dark antique furniture, nostalgic scenes of English country life or carnage wrecked on English offices and their wives by mutineering Indians We are also shown the lounge with its tiger and leopard trophies. God knows how many big cats have been shot over the years. The dining room is grand, if a little gloomy, and the large table is full of strange objects and silver ware. Lunch was also rather strange – chicken salad that seemed to have been bulked out with Saltine biscuits. On the various sideboards there were other weird objects, including a coffee grinder and a patent decongestant machine with an obscene perished rubber nozzle. Jim is convinced that they should take a bulldozer to all these crumbling Raj buildings.

We bid farewell to Michael and Mary and go shopping Scharlie buys enough

Lunch at Mary and Michael's hotel, the Carlton Plaisance

blankets to open a stall on the market in Cambridge. We find a shop that sells fine shawls in silk, wool or viscose and buy silk scarves and some lacquer boxes for the children. The Rice Bowl serves simple wholesome food – clear soups, noodles and steamed dumplings stuffed with vegetables or chicken. It is good, so good in fact that we go back there every night sampling different parts of the extensive menu of Tibetan, Thai and Chinese cuisine. The waiter is an Indian with a gentle polite smile. He says that they have two cooks – one Thai and one Chinese.

We enjoy our daily walks along The Mall to the other end of town past Tibetan stallholders, immaculately dressed, but selling cheap clothes to the locals. Every night they pack away their wares in tin trunks and every morning they roll out the blue awnings and them attach with ropes to the hillside. We pass the sellers of wooden objects and decorated bags into the busy end of town full of small thriving shops and food stalls. At night it becomes a magical place of light and colour of the dirt and the crumbling buildings are invisible. We find a shop that sells wonderful quality Kashmir goods that even Jim and Steve are tempted into buying presents. The shopkeeper is intelligent informed and relaxed in his sales technique. We feel at home here and the place begins

School children on the Mall

to look familiar with people we recognise. Jim even forgives our hotel because of the leisurely breakfasts we take on the wide veranda – fruit juice and fried eggs and marmalade, tea and toast, and newspapers to read.

Thursday 21 September

We move hotel today. Over breakfast Scharlie was intrigued with the Warli paintings and got the manager to show her the full set. Two of his paintings – white on black – are for sale and she asked how much he wants for them. It looks as if we are bound for another large purchase. We arrange to return tomorrow if we decide to go ahead and can get the rupees he needs. We have our bags carried down the zigzag path to the road a few hundred feet below the hotel because the taxi can't get through. We have only Rs.50 in small notes to tip the two men, one of whom has been our waiter. So the following day, when I go back I give him 100.

The taxi is a beat up Ambassador and we only just managed to fit in. Jim's head touches the ceiling and there is a worn spot above the driver's head. These cars are obviously designed for comfort of the passengers in the back

Jim and Scharlie on the terrace of the Padmini Nivas

seat, not the chauffeur. The rooms are nice – better than the ones they showed me earlier. It is very misty and cold and we hear music outside. The room has a large bay window with seating. Outside we can see that there is a school sports day in progress. Parents are seated in a marquee and the concrete play area has been decorated with flower petals. Half a dozen young women in red saris are dancing. They're doing the same steps the girls did in the school in Lata. They are so graceful – their hands and gestures so expressive, their hip movements so suggestive. Then it is the turn of the younger children and finally an endless series of roller-skating feats. The children in pale green shirts seemed to be much better than the others. They are all very slim and athletic and seem to have the technique of taking the bends fast. We watch for a while, and then go for lunch.

That afternoon we walk up to the Kasmanda Palace for tea. Scharlie and Jim want to see it. It's foggy but despite the weather we opt for tea in the garden and chat. The staff look on in wonder at the mad English. Finally the heavens open and drive us indoors. We order more tea in the conservatory and examine the photographs of English Viceroys with assembled Maharajahs and Princes. They are fascinating in a way – one white-haired man in a solar

Trophies on the staircase of the Kasmanda Place Hotel, 1836 (photo Siddharth Gaur)

topee ruling over an Empire. We are shown the Royal suites and the trophy lounge. There are huge buffalo heads and a rhino on the wall above the main stairs. The smallest is a stuffed hispidhare –now extinct!

Our final meal at the Rice Bowl is something of a blowout. Our friendly waiter has persuaded us to go for a full meal. It looks like an enormous amount, but in fact is so well cooked it seems light and we finish it all. Scharlie has fallen in love with the cows that wander the streets. They seem to belong to no one and everyone and subsist like the dogs on refuse and handouts. But like the people, all the animals seem most placid and content. No one here this maltreats animals and it shows. There are rhesus monkeys everywhere. They play on the roofs and telegraph wires and go around in troops with a large dominant male. There was an old male sitting on a wall contemplating the world. He looked as though he had been usurped but in this benign environment was able to live out his life in happy contemplation. Once a leopard would have had him, but the only sign of leopard we'd had was high up near Nanda Devi. We get a good nights sleep and go and see the man about the paintings.

Friday 22 September

We have managed to get the money we needed last night. Passing a travel agent we asked if he would change money. We borrowed money from Jim and went back to see him before he closed. The road was slippery from the rain and Steve's shoes didn't grip well, so as he steadied myself to step across the board over the drain into the shop, his feet went from under him and he skateboarded into the shop. The grey-haired Sikh was most put out and got Steve water and a cloth to wash himself, surprised that he had not injured himself more.

Our man was waiting for us on the veranda of the hotel with the paintings rolled in a plastic tube. He seemed pleased to see us and we ordered breakfast and sat on the terrace. Then back to the Horizon at other end of town. We have walked up and down the Mall a few times. On the way we checked out the booking office. It was cleaner inside than the outside suggested and a notice informed us we could get a discount on our ticket

So Steve has to go to the hotel, get the ticket and return to the booking office – all before our taxi arrives. He queues behind a group of Tibetans only to discover that our tickets are non-refundable travel vouchers. Still we are in good time for the taxi, and even manage a coffee and chat with the manager of the hotel before loading the small Japanese car and setting off. Although the car looks small it has a roof rack and is much more comfortable and feels safer than the Ambassador taxis. The first section to Dehra Dun is an endless series of zigzag curves through cool green-forested slopes. Pretty soon Steve feels carsick and Jim kindly offers to swap to let him in the front. I splash water on my face, swill my mouth out and we're off again. We stop at a checkpoint on the state border and our driver goes off to parlay with the soldiers. One pokes his head in our window and asked if we have air conditioning. We say no. He seems unconvinced. Our driver returns and announces we have to pay tax. Jim is put out and feels he should have been told. Nevertheless he forks out a Rs.500 note, but doesn't get any change. No one else is stopped. We wonder what it's all about; maybe the car isn't taxed for out-of-state hire.

After Dehra Dun we travel through endless fields and ribbon development – endless plantations of mango, teak and sugarcane punctuated by noisy dusty towns that look like hell, but all we see I see are laughing, lovely people. The

Main road out of Mussoorie

road is extraordinary. It is the main road from the north, yet it is only single carriageway and full of potholes. Yet maybe most of the roads in India are like this. It is used by everything – big Tata lorries and buses, down to rickshaws and bicycles. There are bullock carts pulling huge loads, led by a rope through the nose, the driver giving directions with a simple flick of the rope. There are lots of tractors hauling stone and gravel. The latter handcrafted by people sitting by the road with hammers. There are strange homemade vehicles with single cylinder water pump motors that chug along about 5 miles an hour. There are lots of motorbikes and scooters, many of them carrying a wife riding sidesaddle, and a child pressed between father and mother. All the motorbikes have a small foot shelf and sari guard on the left-hand side so the women can sit sideways. And of course there is the occasional car trying to fight its way through this mayhem, but being brought to a sharp halt every few hundred yards by multiple sleeping policemen or by deep potholes that the drivers try and weave around. This obviously lowers the speed, which is just as well since the only way to overtake is to jink out in the face of oncoming traffic and in again immediately to avoid a head-on collision – all to the blurring of horns. No one uses a mirror and they rely on the person behind honking and on delicate hand signals from front see passenger indicating whether it is possible or unwise to pull out.

We go through some crowded centres, but there is nothing to distinguish one place from the next and very few road signs. The roadside vegetable stalls are most carefully arranged, but the general impression one gets is of dirt and squalor, much aggravated by all things connected with keeping these ramshackle vehicles on the road. We see a number of roadside repairs going on, with men crouched on huge truck axles, wheels scattered about like coins. Behind the continuous ribbon of shacks and brick shops, there is the countryside with green fields of sugarcane and fruit trees. Everywhere there are people working – planting out tree whips or hoeing the rich soil. We notice tall beehive like structures about 3m tall all tied about with woven rope. We see women patting cow dung into cakes to dry for fuel. It seems the fresh dung is moulded into a pile and covered with leaves before being formed into these cakes. Maybe it is necessary to compost the dung to kill the microbes. Anyway, like so much we've seen, it's a mystery. How can a nation like India move forward without better roads, asks Jim. We are beginning to regret coming by car.

It is nearly 3pm and we are hungry and tired and we haven't found the promised restaurant that our hotel manager recommended – the Cheetral. Then we see signs and eventually we are there. Jim says he would prefer a roadside stall but this turns out to be a good choice. We find a cool table outside under the trees. The service is fantastic food is good, the prices low and the loos clean and modern. Twenty minutes and we are off again. It starts to get dark when we are still 20 or 30 km from Delhi. The Friday evening traffic is heavy and our driver announces he doesn't know the way. We hit the ring road but none of us has any frame of reference to help find the way. He seems to have lost his confidence and we go slower and slower. We think we may have taken a wrong turning, but we press on. We miss the turn we have been told about and are forced to continue on the ring road. Scharlie and Jim are getting more and more agitated in the back and Scharlie takes to calling people over for directions, which further undermines our driver's confidence. However, the repeated instructions are beginning to make sense. We see a sign for a turnoff to India Gate near Connaught Place and Steve recognises the colonial architecture of the outer circle. Our driver wants to drop us here, but we persuade him to continue, hoping we will recognise the turnoff to the hotel. Jim is not convinced, so we stop and ask someone. No one seems to recognise the name of our hotel, perhaps it's our pronunciation, so with an inspired thought Steve asks for the bus station, which he knows is near our hotel and people point up the road. Finally we are there and it's only a little after 7.30. It suddenly doesn't seem so bad after all. Jim hands over the money. We feel sorry for him. He found it hard coming to the big city and now has to find his way back home in his own in the dark. Perhaps he will park up and sleep. We give him a little more money and check-in.

Our room is next Anna and Phil, who we discover got in 10 minutes ahead of us. They have collected our carpet so can pack it tonight. It is huge and very heavy. We're going to be overweight by a lot. We shower and change into clean clothes and meet in the lobby to go out to eat. Jim knows a place call the Pumpkin and a Sikh taxi driver offers to take us. He also arranges to take Jim to the airport for an early flight and return for us later. It suddenly all seems easy. We manage to get the carpet and everything else into our two cases, with heavier books in our hand luggage.

The restaurant is good – lively and modern with a salad bar and all-day breakfast menu, plus alcohol! We have a jolly time exchanging stories. Phil and Anna have had a rough time travelling to Agra and Jaipur. Their driver was on a mission to maximise his commission and took them to places that were unfriendly and poor value, including a home-stay that served crisps and tomato sauce for breakfast. Jaipur was a real shock to the system, said Anna teeming with poor people, and everywhere you go you are assaulted by touts and beggars. But the Taj Mahal is all it's cracked up to be. Phil was also much taken by the huge sundial, which as well as telling the time with an accuracy of 20 seconds, also indicated the position of all the planets and constellations. We also managed to do a great deal of shopping, said Phil. So much in fact that Anna has been shedding clothes she bought earlier and when we leave the hotel tomorrow has to give the room service a signed letter handing over the dresses she is leaving so the maid won't be accused of stealing them.

Delhi

Saturday 23 September

The bellhop helps weigh our bags; one bag weighs 17 kg and the other 37kg. So we are 15kg overweight. We remember we need to buy biscuits for the office and Scharlie wants to find a Bo leaf. So we leave the bags, having tipped the bellhop, and set off towards Connaught Place. A chuck chuck driver most insistently wants to take us in the opposite direction, saying we are walking the wrong way for the bazaars. But we are hardened travellers and brush him off with a polite but firm goodbye and walk on. Next to the bus station there are two Bo trees and just beyond a stall selling nice biscuits. On the way back Steve pulls down a branch and Scharlie harvests her leaves.

The taxi arrives and amazingly everything fits in and we have an easy trip to the airport. Scharlie is caught short and has to rush to the loo, leaving Steve to take the baggage through security. He is feeling really ill now, and has a severe headache. The check-in girl wants the other passenger and says the bag with the carpet is too heavy and that we will have to repack. Steve unzips the North Face holdall, takes out a rucksack, repacks and rejoins the check-in queue. It's all very tiresome, but we should have known better. Steve is grumpy and not very nice to Scharlie, which makes him feel worse. He decides just to be quiet and try to get through the day.

We are hanging about and Steve drifts into a bookshop having a large note left and sees a thick Penguin on Indian religions. It is on the top shelf and in reaching up for it he brings the whole lot down, which the shop manager and he somehow managed to catch. He hands the remaining cash, then realises it's not enough. Quick as a flash the shopkeeper says he can take sterling and give change. He whips out his calculator, takes the Rs 100 note and two fivers and gives back £3.50 in change!

We go through customs and have the usual long wait, but it doesn't seem so bad. The departure hall is cool and uncrowded and people are relaxed and it's all very civilised. We have two more security checks and then we board. The seats are tight, but the service is great and the plane is spanking new. Only British customs to negotiate with our truckload of merchandise. We'll breeze through the nothing to declare channel and just hope we don't look too guilty.

How to pull reflections of a trip like this together? We seem to have been away from England forever, yet it's only three weeks. Have our travels? As we said to Mary on our walk, spiritual awareness, like happiness, comes fleetingly – a smile, a generous act, a conversation shared, all have significance. And there is something about the slow speed of movement, the constantly changing view and the clarity and complexity of the natural world that salves the soul. There is something about finding your way in mountainous country that is similar in all wild places. And for different reasons, Scharlie and I feel at home in the hills. So did we experience anything more than we would have climbing in the Lakes, Scotland or the Alps? The experience in India was distinct, but it is hard to put one's finger on why. It is tempting to say it's the size and grandeur that obviously dwarfs anything in Britain. Or one might say it's the Indian cultural experience. But I think it may be as simple as the courtesy and sensitivity of people we met. It would be nice to have the opportunity to come back to the Himalayas but if we don't manage to we will always remember this trip with great affection.

Nanda Devi